RUTH AND ESTHER

WOMEN OF AGENCY AND ADVENTURE

BRUCE G. EPPERLY

Energion Publications
Gonzalez, FL
2016

ISBN10: 1-63199-219-8
ISBN13: 978-1-63199-219-3

Energion Publications
P. O. Box 841
Gonzalez, FL 32560
850-525-3916

energion.com
pubs@energion.com

With gratitude to the members of

South Congregational Church, United Church of Christ,

Centerville, Massachusetts

for their love of learning and support of my scholarly adventures

ONCE UPON A TIME IN THE MIDDLE EAST

I was surprised when my Bible study classes at South Congregational Church chose to read the books of Ruth and Esther. Most Christians know virtually nothing about these texts. At first glance, they contain no doctrinal statements, ethical admonitions, or prophetic challenges. There are no mighty acts of God or miracles, and no great demonstrations of divine sovereignty. In fact, at first glance, God appears to be on the sidelines or, in the case of the Protestant and Jewish texts of the book of Esther, not even mentioned. Ruth and Esther are cited only three times in the three-year lectionary cycle of the church. We know Ruth primarily from her declaration of loyalty to Naomi, and though her pledge is to her mother-in-law, it is primarily invoked at weddings. Although the Book of Esther is at the heart of the Jewish Purim celebrations, the only time I have heard it quoted in Christian contexts involves Mordecai's counsel to Esther, suggesting she was elevated to queen for "just such a time as this."

There is no clear historical evidence that either woman existed, nor do we know with exactness the authorship or dating of either text. It is easy to think of these texts as interesting novellas or short stories with little importance for our own faith journeys. But, like all good literature, both the books of Ruth and Esther are filled with surprising wisdom and unexpected theological reflection that goes far beyond superficial readings.

Ruth and Esther are women of agency and adventure. They are aliens, whose pilgrimages were, to some extent, against their will or in conflict with their life plans. They were resourceful and proactive women in patriarchal cultures, in which women depended on the support of males to survive. Both women were aliens who faced the possibility of death and destruction as a result of circumstances beyond their control. One became wealthy and powerful as queen, the other the spouse of wealthy landowner, but both were subject to the apparently arbitrary decisions of males with authority. Both women were agents in their destiny fulfilling their vocations in their particular culture. The impact of their decisions shaped the destiny of the Jewish people. Ruth and Esther were loyal to causes greater than self-interest, and their loyalty inspired resourcefulness and perhaps cunning to save those they loved.

The Protestant Reformer Martin Luther had a low estimate of the book of Esther as a result of the absence of God language in the Hebrew text, and wondered if it should remain in scripture. In contrast to much of scripture, the book of Ruth also appears to place God in the backseat in its focus on human agency. Still, the stories of these two women, called to shape their people's destinies, reveal the gentle providence of God at every step and are appropriate texts for our pluralistic, postmodern age. For most of us living in the twenty-first century, God seldom announces God's coming with "thus says the Lord" or "I am a messenger of God" or "I'm telling you what to do." In our contemporary experience, God's movements are much more subtle, and are found in intuitions, hunches, dreams, synchronous encounters, and insights. Ruth and Esther experienced God in the same way. They discovered God's guidance in their quest to be faithful to their loved ones and secure survival for themselves and others. God is with them, as we will discover, each step of the way, presenting options and possibilities and calling them to go beyond self-interest to care for the well-being of others.

Ruth and Esther are timely books for us. They remind us that we can be faithful to God's calling in challenging circumstances and discover our calling even though the pathway ahead is uncharted and uncertain. The hiddenness of divine activity makes these two books important spiritual reading for individuals and churches today. Even active Christians and spiritual leaders seldom receive divine operating instructions for our congregations and personal lives, and must rely on God's guidance to emerge as we make decisions about the future. Like Ruth and Esther, there are no guarantees that we will clearly experience God's vision or the paths we should take. In fact, even when we are most certain of our faith and calling, humility demands the recognition that we could be wrong. But, in their spirit, we will discover that we can only know by the walking. In this adventurous spirit, let us begin our journey with a prayer from John Henry Newman:

Lead, Kindly Light, amid the encircling gloom,
Lead Thou me on!
The night is dark, and I am far from home,
Lead Thou me on!
Keep Thou my feet; I do not ask to see
The distant scene; one step enough for me.

RUTH'S UNEXPECTED ADVENTURE

CHAPTER 1

STRANGERS IN A STRANGE LAND

Immigration has always been a social and political issue. It is also a religious issue insofar as the immigrant challenges us to see God's presence in the wholly — or is it holy? — other. Recently, scores of demonstrators waved signs and shouted expletives at children and teenagers who had, with the encouragement of anguished parents, immigrated to the United States from Central America to seek safety from the poverty and gang violence of their homelands. Four centuries before that time, the pilgrim parents sailed to North America, seeking religious and economic freedom. They saw themselves as heirs to the children of Israel, whose exodus from slavery in Egypt took them to freedom in God's land of milk and honey, Canaan.

Immigration means hardship and is usually undertaken as a last resort, when all other options have been explored. Immigrants, in ancient times and today, face antagonism and prejudice. They have to adapt to a new language and culture, and often have to start over again economically and professionally. In the spirit of Robert Heinlein's novel, they are truly strangers in a strange land.

The Book of Ruth is an immigration story. Once upon a time, there was a famine in Bethlehem, "the house of bread," and a certain man Elimelech, his wife Naomi, and their two sons, Mahlon and Chilion, sojourn to Moab. The journey must have been difficult physically, spiritually, and emotionally. Their roots and property were in Bethlehem and they were going to a land, whose relationships with the children of Israel, were complicated and conflict-ridden. In Israelite lore, the Moabites were the children of an incestuous relationship between Lot and his daughters. Moreover, they worshiped a god who sometimes demanded child sacrifice. Further, the Moabites were also known to be sexually promiscuous by Israelite standards. The children of Israel and Moabites often engaged in military conflicts. Elimelech and Naomi must have been desperate to leave their homeland and settle in such an unfriendly region, among people most Jews saw as moral and religious inferiors. It was a matter of survival.

Famine was, and still is, a matter of life and death. World Vision asserts that 2.6 million children die of hunger each year. Other relief organizations estimate that the number of hunger-related deaths among children, in a world that has enough food for everyone, may be as high as ten million. Like so many people then and now, Elimelech and Naomi left their home, property, and friends not only for a better life but also for the survival of their two children.

We don't know how Elimelech and Naomi fared in Moab. Lacking suitable mates from their own ethnic community, the boys settled for Moabite wives. I am sure Elimelech and Naomi were initially disappointed at the son's choices and hoped that neither bride would fit the stereotypical promiscuity of Moabite women. But, there were no other options, and so the boys married Ruth and Orpah. The family survived, but never prospered. Then, tragedy struck. One by one the males died, leaving Naomi to face the future, childless and with two childless daughters-in-law.

Naomi sets off toward home because, as an outsider in Moab, she has nowhere else to go. Naomi urges her daughters-in-law, Ruth and Orpah, to return home. She is aware that they will be strangers and perhaps looked down upon in Bethlehem. She is equally aware that they will be two more mouths to feed and that as childless, Moabite, and possibly barren, their prospects for marriage and economic security will be dim in Bethlehem.

The text notes without any sense of judgment that Orpah returns to her kinfolk. Ruth protests Naomi's decision, and vows to be with her mother-in-law till they are parted by death.

Do not press me to leave you
or to turn back from following you!
Where you go, I will go;
where you lodge, I will lodge;
your people shall be my people,
and your God my God.
Where you die, I will die—
there will I be buried.
May the Lord do thus and so to me,
and more as well,
if even death parts me from you!

— Ruth 1:16–17

Ruth's vow is an act of love that crosses the borders of time, place, religion, and ethnicity. It is an act, first of all, to insure their survival. Two women alone will not survive the rigors of the wilderness, nor will the elder Naomi be able to make a living or find a spouse in her homeland apart from a partner. She has a piece of property, whose ownership jeopardized by the death of her husband and sons, but no one to tend it. Perhaps, Ruth also realizes that she cannot go home again. Childless and the widow of a foreigner, she may no longer be welcome in her parents' home. More importantly, Ruth's vow is steadfast and loving. Ruth's fidelity mirrors God's unconditional commitment to humankind. God's loving-kindness delivered the Hebrews from slavery and insured their survival in the land of Canaan, and Ruth's vow will insure survival for Naomi and the family line of Elimelech.

Ruth and Naomi create a new kind of family. Two women are bound together by marriage, survival, and mutual respect and affection.

Ruth's vow reminds us that relationships are holistic and multi-dimensional. Our vows take place amid the economic and relational dimensions of life. Friendships and marriages encompass more than good times and romance. They embrace the well-being of in-laws, children and grandchildren, and the day to day realities of making a living and insuring the well-being of the next generation. When my wife and I married in 1979, we had no idea that our marriage would involve the care and companionship of my mother-in-law for sixteen years and, now in our sixties, spending nearly every afternoon with two young boys, while their parents are at work. The greatest gift is love, and a deep and abiding love embraces every aspect of life from diapers to Depends!

Ruth's vow to become an ethnic and spiritual pilgrim is filled with risk. Will she be accepted as a stranger in a strange land? Will the locals shun her, believing all the stereotypes about Moabite women? Will she have resourcefulness to make a new life economically for herself and Naomi? Will any man accept her in marriage, given her ethnicity, apparent barrenness, and widowed status? As the story unfolds, these mysteries will be revealed along with the quiet and gentle providence of God, whose love embraces the foreigner, widow, and impoverished.

CHAPTER 2
A FEMALE "JOB"?

Every person of faith has to come to terms with the reality of suffering. A twelve-year-old is shot for no good reason on the streets of a major American city, a roof collapses at a concert killing dozens, a family on its way to celebrate Christmas with friends is killed by a drunk driver, a bomb goes off at a mosque in Iraq, and a tidal wave kills thousands. This past summer my best friend died of cancer, despite my daily intercessions on her behalf, and in the past year, two of my oldest high school friends have also been claimed by cancer. My son was diagnosed with cancer shortly after his wedding and although he is a survivor with two young children, I can still recall my feelings of fear and hopelessness. Life is difficult for the good and evil alike.

The biblical tradition takes the reality of suffering seriously. Suffering is not an illusion, but a reality that shapes the lives of persons and nations. The greatness of the scriptural tradition is its willingness to confront suffering head on, avoid superficial explanations, and explore many possible explanations. On the one hand, the biblical tradition proclaims that God is sovereign, the creator of heaven and earth. Life and death, healing and sickness, alike come from the hand of God. On the other hand, suffering is seen as the result of divine punishment for human misdeeds. People reap what they sow; the righteous flourish and the evil perish. The book of Job challenges both of these explanations: in protesting against his undeserved suffering, Job discovers that the righteous suffer in a world shaped by chance events as well as divine wisdom.[1]

Centuries later Jesus was asked if a man's blindness resulted from his or his parents' sinfulness. Jesus answer was a clear "no." Inspired by his loving relationship to his Father, Jesus challenged images of divine punishment and called his followers to work to alleviate suffering whenever the opportunity arises (John 9:1–7).

---

1 For more on the book of Job, see Bruce Epperly, *Finding God in Suffering: A Journey with Job* (Gonzales, FL: Energion, 2014).

In contrast to acts-consequences understandings of suffering, Jesus asserted that God seeks abundant life for all and that the sun and rain, positive and negative events, fall equally on the righteous and unrighteous. (See John 10:10 and Matthew 5:43–45.) Our world reveals both chance and divine wisdom. The sufferings we experience can result from sinful and destructive behaviors; they can also emerge from catastrophic health incidents or wayward cells.[2]

Naomi also struggles with the reality of suffering. In a world in which she believes God is in control, she has lost her husband and sons, her identity as a wife, place in the community, and virtually all her financial resources. She wonders if she will survive without the kindness of strangers. One author describes Naomi as a "female Job," given the severity of her losses.[3]

Naomi's words are reminiscent of the protests of Job and the Psalmist, both of whom feel acutely both the absence and malevolence of God. Why have you forsaken me, O God? What have I done to deserve the deaths of my loved ones and the loss of security and status? Was my sojourn in Moab really so heinous to deserve the death sentence for my sons and husband? Perhaps she even wondered if her son's marriages to "degenerate" Moabite women contributed to their deaths. Listen to Naomi's words, addressed directly to the townsfolk of Bethlehem and indirectly to God.

> *Call me no longer Naomi [the pleasant one],*
> *Call me Mara [the bitter],*
> *The Almighty has dealt bitterly with me.*
> *I went away full, but the Lord has brought me back empty;*
> *Why call me Naomi when the Lord has dealt harshly with me,*
> *The Almighty has brought calamity on me.*
>
> — Ruth 1:20–21

Naomi believes that God is the source of her anguish, either through the arbitrariness and inscrutability of divine providence or divine punishment for her family's sojourn in Moab and son's

---

2 For more a theological reflection on the relationship of God and suffering, see Bruce Epperly, *Process Theology: Embracing Adventure with God* (Gonzales, FL: Energion Publications, 2014).

3 Carolyn Custis James, *The Gospel of Ruth: Loving God Enough to Break the Rules* (Grand Rapids; Zondervan, 2008).

marriage to Moabite women. Naomi protests that God has "dealt bitterly," "dealt harshly," and "brought calamity." Like Job, Naomi does not deny God's existence; her concern is God's character. With what kind of God are we dealing? Is God for us or against us? Does my well-being matter to God? Will God restore my fortunes and give me hope for the future in the form of grandchildren to carry on the family name? Despite the fact that the author of the book of Ruth sees God moving within the tragedies of life to bring new life to Naomi, Ruth, and the lineage of Elimelech, the possibility God's restorative grace is initially more than Naomi can fathom.

The book of Ruth, similar to Psalm 23, reminds us that must go "through" and not "around" the darkest valleys. In the midst of the journey, there is no guarantee of a positive outcome; but in the spirit of the poem "Footprints in the Sand," God is carrying us when we feel most alone and vulnerable. God is making a way, as we shall discover, when we can see nothing but a dead end.

Naomi's protests, like the lamentations of Job and the Psalms, remind us that our grief needs to be expressed. Our honest expression of feelings is an act of trust in God's companionship and the compassion of others. We can take of feelings of loss, anger, and grief to the One to whom all hearts are open and all desires known. The problem of evil can never fully be solved intellectually or theologically, but we can find healing in the midst of pain by opening our hearts to God and one another. We can also respond to the suffering we and others experience by positive and life-supporting actions. This is the wisdom of the book of Ruth.

CHAPTER 3
THE ECONOMICS OF LOVE

A relative of mine once told her daughter, "If you fall in love, you might as well fall in love with a wealthy farmer." At first glance, that's exactly what happened in the story of Ruth and Boaz. A beautiful widow, down on her luck, meets a wealthy farmer. There are family ties and mutual attraction. There are also impediments to their match; there is another potential suitor and the couple come from different, and often antagonistic, ethnic groups. Naomi hatches a plan to cement their relationship, and they live happily and prosperously ever after. Love conquers all!

Is an enduring love really that easy? Does falling in love really solve all of our problems? Or, does it create new challenges that inspire us to be our most resourceful, compassionate, and persistent selves?

In the twenty-first century, marriage focuses on romance and attraction. But, after over thirty-five years of marriage, I realize that marriage is multi-dimensional in nature and purpose. Marriage invites us to be faithful through all the seasons of life. The words of the traditional marriage vow capture the holistic nature of marriage:

For better, for worse.
For richer, for poorer.
In sickness and in health.
To love and to cherish
Till death do us part.[4]

Over the course of our marriage, my wife and I have dealt with a child diagnosed with cancer, economic uncertainty due to professional downsizing, challenging careers, and care for a mentally ill brother and a dying mother. Now, in our sixties, our marriage embraces the lives of our son and daughter-in-law and two young

---

4 The alternative "as long as we both shall live" says virtually the same thing, but on their joyous marriage day many couples shy away from the reality that every healthy long-term marriage eventually involves some form of diminishment and death.

children, who spend most weekday afternoons and a night or two a week at our home. Marriage is about romance, but it is also about nurturing a family, caring for the sick, facing tragedy together, and economic well-being and survival. In the latter case, just ask the husband who works 14 hours a day at two jobs, neither of which provide more than $10 an hour to support his wife and family, or the wife and mother who must work a second shift at the diner after the death of her husband.

Ruth and Naomi are bound by love, but also the survival. Ruth's vow encompasses her love for her mother-in-law and her willingness to change her religious tradition and leave her homeland; it also means doing her best to secure economic stability for two women on their own in a society where men held the purse strings and property rights.

There is a social safety net, but it is modest and unpredictable. When Ruth goes to Boaz's fields to glean, she is not only depending on the kindness of strangers; she is also relying on the wealthy farmer following God's law and the community's social practice. The practice of gleaning, or leaving the edges of the field uncut or the fallen sheaves on the field, was put in place as part of Israel's social compact with "the alien, the orphan, and the widow" (Leviticus 19:9–10; 23:22; Deuteronomy 24:19–23). According to scripture, concern for the poor is not optional, it is a requirement of God, built into the social structure. When Israel turns its back on the poor, as the prophets Amos and Hosea warn, the nation will collapse and there will be a famine of hearing the word of God (Amos 8:1–12).

Despite the practice of gleaning, Naomi and Ruth are still in economic peril. Like the working poor of our nation, and today's migrant workers many of which are undocumented immigrants, they live from harvest to harvest and paycheck to paycheck. They must find something more stable and this involves finding a husband for Ruth. Thinking of their well-being as a social unit, Naomi counsels Ruth in words that join economics and romance.

Naomi her mother-in-law said to her, "My daughter, I need to seek some security for you, so that it may be well with you. Now here is our kinsman Boaz, with whose young women you have been working. See, he is winnowing barley tonight at the threshing floor. Now wash and anoint yourself, and put on your best clothes and go down to the threshing floor; but do not make yourself known to the man until he has finished eating and drinking. When he lies down, observe the place where he lies; then, go and uncover his feet and lie down; and he will tell you what to do."

— Ruth 3:1–4

Ruth risks her reputation and possibly her life to secure economic well-being for Naomi and herself. The reader only needs to recall the concern both Boaz and Naomi have that Ruth would be sexually harassed or physically harmed in the fields. Although Boaz has a reputation for being a good man, there is no guarantee that he will be a gentleman after a few drinks, treat Ruth with respect, and honor her integrity and economic well-being. One night stands and rapes have occurred throughout history and are even recorded within the pages of scripture.

Power relationships, whether in economics, race, or gender, matter. In light of the recent killings of African American youth by law enforcement officers, many church leaders, both black and white, are proclaiming "black lives matter." The book of Ruth proclaims "Moabite lives matter," "foreign women matter," "women's lives matter," "widows' lives matter," and "economically disadvantaged lives matter."

Hidden beneath the romance is the quest for a just social order, akin to the prophetic challenges to the Southern and Northern kingdoms of Israel. While seldom put in practice, Israel enshrined both the sabbatical and jubilee years, intended to redistribute wealth so that the poor and vulnerable would have a fair shake (Leviticus 25:8–13; 20–22). Moreover, the prophets proclaim that our ability to worship God and hear God's word in our lives is related to our care, personally and corporately, for the economically disadvantaged. God says to those who perpetrate structures of injustice that lead to poverty and foreclosures:

I hate, I despise your festivals,
And I take no delight in your solemn assemblies....
Take away from me the noise of your songs;
I will not listen to the melody of your harps.

But, let justice roll down like waters,
And righteousness like an ever-flowing stream.
— Amos 5:21, 23–24

The book Ruth takes place during "the days when the judges ruled" (Ruth 1:1). This was an era of violence and polarization, and by implication, economic injustice and insecurity. The realities of famine — starvation and poverty — led to death and forced immigration. Yet, the book of Ruth seems, as some scholars suggest, to be an island of civility, compassion, and care, in a tumultuous time. The book of Ruth points us toward a different set of values, which embrace the well-being of others. Despite its patriarchal context, the book of Ruth tells us clearly that the poor and vulnerable are our business. Our well-being and the future of the nation — after all, Ruth is David's great grandmother — depend on how we respond to those at economic and social margins and to the strangers in our midst. The apparently hidden God of the book of Ruth is present in the barley field and threshing floor and in the challenges widows face. Centuries later, Jesus was to suggest that our care for others shapes God's own experiences of the world, for "as you have done unto to the least of these who are members of my family, you did unto me" (Matthew 25:40).

CHAPTER 4
SEIZING THE MOMENT

Agency leads to surprise and adventure. In the book of Ruth, the three main characters take charge of their lives and alter their circumstances. They don't wait for external events to determine their destinies. They make decisions that shape their own futures and, unknown to them, the future a nation.

Despite her grief and anger at God, Naomi refuses to accept her life circumstances as predestined and unalterable. She believes that change can happen and life can be better, despite her bitterness and anger against God. She leaves Moab to face an uncertain future in her homeland. There are no guarantees, but she presses forward with her doubts and depression, hoping for new life in Bethlehem. Naomi urges Ruth to reach out to Boaz, and provides instructions for Ruth's tryst with Boaz. Naomi knows that she who hesitates is lost. Perhaps, she sees a spark between Ruth and Boaz and wants to capitalize on their relationship to secure the well-being of Ruth and herself.

Ruth also is an agent of her destiny. While Orpah heads for her family home, Ruth presses forward to Bethlehem, guided by a vow and a vision of hope. Her loyalty to Naomi is her polestar, empowering her to start over again and take risks to secure her mother-in-law's well-being. Despite the fact she is childless, and presumed infertile, in a culture where childlessness is seen as a curse from God, jeopardizing future marital prospects, Ruth takes a chance. She reaches out to Boaz, hopeful that by their relationship new life can emerge from barrenness.

Ruth takes a chance on marriage. Her mother urges Ruth to meet Boaz after dark, initiate a relationship, and then let him tell her what to do. Ruth takes a different course. After settling down with Boaz, she proposes marriage to him, inviting him to fulfill his destiny as Elimelech's next of kin and her family line's redeemer (3:9). She risks rejection to invite Boaz to a possibility he may not previously have imagined.

Boaz also takes charge. Surprised by Ruth's presence and proposal, which he willingly accepts, he goes into action, finding the actual next of kin, who by rights has first call to purchase Elimelech's property, and making him an offer he has to refuse.

The book of Ruth is a testimony to the synergy of divine providence and human agency. As we shall see, God remains anonymous throughout the book. Moreover, nothing in the text is predestined or determined in advance. The future is open and waiting for us to act. God does not plan the details of our lives in advance, nor is God jealous of human initiative. The more we do in terms of personal creativity, the more God is able to do to positively shape history. From the initiative of Ruth, Boaz, and Naomi, a boy child is born who is the grandparent of David, the greatest king of Israel. Divine providence encourages humans to make decisions that will shape their futures.

The book of Ruth describes ordinary people, who by their faithfulness, bring about extraordinary things. Ruth challenges us to make decisions, go beyond our comfort zones, and see ourselves as God's partners in creating the future.

Many Christians are content to sit on the sidelines, expecting a divine rescue operation or using the words, "God's will," to excuse them from involvement in changing their communities and the world. They look for a "second coming," that will solve all their problems. In withdrawing from history, they turn their backs on the wisdom of the book of Ruth. The book of Ruth suggests that against all odds, we can change history. The future is open and depends on our actions to bring healing to our communities and our planet. In fact, when we move forward, we become God's companions and co-workers in making a way where there was previously a dead end.

Every USA president has quotes to remember. Ronald Reagan affirmed, "We can't help everyone, but everyone can help someone." Abraham Lincoln said, "In the end, it's not the years of your life that count, but the life in your years." And, appropriate to the book of Ruth, Barack Obama affirmed, "Change will not happen if we wait for some other person or wait for some other time. We are the ones we have been waiting for. We are the change that we seek."

Ruth, Boaz, and Naomi are God's agents of destiny. They bring about the changes they seek by their fidelity, loyalty, and love and initiative. Their example inspires us to be agents, sharing in God's holy adventure in our time.

CHAPTER 5
HIDDEN PROVIDENCE

How could a Moabite woman, whose people were looked down upon as spiritually and morally inferior become the great grandmother of Israel's greatest king? According to some Jewish laws, Moabites weren't even allowed to worship with Jews. Mixed marriages were seen as a betrayal of God's plan for the nation and the children of mixed marriages such as Obed and later David were viewed as ethnic inferiors. The book of Ruth challenged racism and ethnic superiority in light of God's providential fidelity.[5]

Fidelity is at the heart of the book of Ruth. Despite appearances to the contrary, God is faithful and will make a way when all we see is a dead end. God is at work in every circumstance of life, quietly and gently acting to bring about God's vision for us and our communities. Divine providence is often hidden but it is always faithful and persistent. Human faithfulness awakens new energies and enables us to move from hopeless passivity to active adventure. When Ruth commits herself to Naomi's well-being, an unexpected pathway to the future emerges for these two vulnerable women and the Jewish people. Ruth's faithfulness creates the possibility that God can be more active in her life and in the history of the Israelite people.

The book of Ruth asserts that divine providence is universal. Perhaps written in response to the quest for ethnic purity, described in the books of Ezra and Nehemiah, both of which commanded Jewish males to divorce their non-Jewish wives, Ruth proclaims that God's providence extends to the much-maligned Moabite and

---

5 Scholars believe that Ruth was written either to affirm that God was present in the calling of David, despite his mixed race heritage, to be the great king of Israel, or that it was a response to edicts in Ezra and Nehemiah, requiring Jews to divorce their foreign wives. (Ezra 9–10) Accordingly, Ruth was written either in the time of David (roughly 1040–970 BCE) to support David's legitimacy and God's universal grace or after the exiles returned to Jerusalem and Israel (roughly 600–500 BCE) to affirm that God works through all people, not just Jews.

to all persons. Ruth is the "good Samaritan" about whom Jesus speaks in his parable. As a Moabite, she is no doubt the object of ethnic stereotypes. Some, no doubt, saw her as loose, promiscuous, and godless. But, she is the embodiment of God's faithfulness in her relationship with Naomi and her continuation of the line of Elimelech and the coming house of David.

God's presence is implicit and understated in the book of Ruth. There are no mighty acts of God, pillars of fire, plagues, or parting waters, and this is the strength of the book. In the spirit of Mother Teresa, following God's vision is not primarily about doing something extraordinary or notable, but faithfully living our day to day lives. God's will seldom addresses us in terms of a command that is clear and obvious. But, in each moment, as the book of Ruth suggests, we are receiving insights, intuitions, hunches and nudges, not to mention synchronous encounters that can change everything if we are attentive and claim our personal agency.

God doesn't choose the events of our lives or our personal gifts and talents in advance. They emerge as we walk the path of faithfulness. One single act of faithfulness, such as Ruth's commitment to Naomi, can change the world. What would have happened if Ruth had chosen to return to her Moabite family? Would David have been born or Israel as a nation seen its greatest moments? Looking further down the line, and from a Christian perspective, would Jesus the Savior have been born in Bethlehem of the lineage of David? At the very least, we can affirm that Ruth's fidelity sets in motion a series of events that secures the line of Elimelech, brings economic well-being to her mother, and makes possible the birth of Obed.

There were no clear pathways for Ruth, nor do we have clear pathways in our own personal, congregational, and community adventures. As the apostle Paul affirms, we see in a mirror dimly and know only in part God's vision (1 Corinthians 13:12). When we say "yes" to God's possibilities and faithfully commit ourselves to others' well-being, we become God's partners in *tikkun'olam*, the healing and transformation of our world.

ESTHER'S TIMELY TRANSFORMATION

CHAPTER 6

THE TWO ESTHERS

The book of Esther describes a pivotal event during the reign of King Ahasuerus, Xerxes I, of Persia (486–465 BCE) in which the Jewish people are delivered from the threat of destruction. While there is no historical evidence that Queen Esther (Ishtar or Hadassah) or Queen Vashti were married to Xerxes I, this ancient tale provides the literary background for the Jewish celebration of Purim and affirms the significance of human agency, courage, and resourcefulness in shaping history in positive ways. Although there is no "original" copy of Esther, just as there are no originals available of any text in the Bible, scholars believe Esther was written sometime between 400–200 BCE.

It might surprise many readers to know that there are two authorized versions of the book of Esther. The Jewish and Protestant traditions follow the Hebrew Masoretic text, while Roman Catholics and Orthodox Christians affirm the somewhat longer Septuagint text, a Greek translation of the Hebrew.[6] It might also surprise the reader that the two translations differ in important ways and serve as type of theological counterbalance to one another.

The Masoretic text, used by most Jews and Protestants, does not mention the name of God. In fact, God's activity is, at first glance, entirely absent from the text. Humans are portrayed as decision-makers and history shapers without God's intervention or

---

6 Translated in the vicinity of 100 years before Jesus' birth, the Septuagint or Greek Old Testament is said to have been the fruit of seventy translators. The Septuagint is often quoted in the New Testament, especially in the letters attributed to the apostle Paul.

guidance. In contrast, the Septuagint text begins with Mordecai's prophetic dream and includes prayers from Esther and Mordecai. God is described as guiding the deliverance of the people by inspiring and responding to the prayers of Esther and Mordecai.

Most scholars suggest that the Masoretic text is likely the earlier of the two. However, recent scholarship has also proposed an "alpha" text as the source of both the Hebrew and Greek texts. While scholarly research may not be important to the average reader, textual studies raise the questions: Was the presence God added to the Greek text or subtracted from the Hebrew text? What was the theological rationale for these processes of addition or subtraction? Does the theological orientation of the texts reflect the Jewish authors' sense of God's presence or absence in their lives?

The Hebrew text, read by Protestants and Jews, focuses on human agency with no apparent divine guidance. Could this have been inspired by Jewish sense of God's absence during the centuries of exile in Babylon and Persia? This same sense of divine absence, and hiddenness, was felt by many Jewish people during the Holocaust. How can God be sovereign or directing history if God's people are being slaughtered? Does the absence of traditional images of God in most people's experiences, despite the realities of pluralism and the proliferation of spiritual movements, reflect our current postmodern world?

Still, the Hebrew text may not be entirely "God-less." Mordecai synchronously hears of a plot against the king and the king, suffering from insomnia, synchronously asks that the annals of his reign be read to him, thus, reminding him of Mordecai's role in saving him from assignation. Moreover, in his counsel to Esther Mordecai implies the movements of a subtle providence that call Esther to act on behalf of her people: "Who knows? Perhaps you have come to royal dignity for such a time as this" (4:14)? If Esther refuses to act, then deliverance may come from "another quarter" (4:13). Could this other quarter be the God of Israel, who has hidden from the people as a result of their injustice and idolatry?

In contrast, the Greek text reflects a more conventional piety in its description of a divine-human call and response in which God is the source of dreams and synchronous events. God also is described in answering the prayers of the faithful, in particular Esther and Mordecai. The piety of the Greek text has led one Hebrew Bible scholar to assert that the theology of the text "makes a theologically ambiguous story [the Hebraic text] into a clear and universal example of the power of conventional piety."[7] Does God show up too quickly, responding directly to the prayers of Mordecai and Esther, in ways that seldom happen in our experience or the experience of most Jews during their exile in Babylon and Persia?[8]

While my own theological sympathies lie with the Hebrew text and its hidden God, I believe that together the texts demonstrate the yin and yang of faith. On the one hand, faith involves taking a risk on God without clear guidance or guarantee of success. Our prayers are often answered subtly, indirectly, or in ways we haven't imagined. On the other hand, spiritual practices open us to greater manifestations of divine providence, revealed in dreams, insights, synchronous encounters, and bursts of redeeming energy that transform persons and historical situations.

Still, I believe the Hebrew version has much to say to spiritual pilgrims today. In light of the Holocaust and killing of over six million Jews, we have to revise our understanding of divine power and revelation. Today, few of us experience explicit divine interventions to change the course of history. We seldom expect God to rescue us from our own mistakes or reverse the course of untreatable cancer, despite our constant intercessions on behalf of friends and family. We don't expect God to destroy our nation's enemies or reverse the damage caused by global climate change. We see ourselves, like Mordecai and Esther, as agents of our own destiny, acting according to our deepest values or most accurate cost-benefit calculations. In contrast to images of God portrayed in *Bruce Almighty* or *Oh, God!*, few people expect God to announce God's presence in any clear and unambiguous way. We go forward one step at a time, trusting the insights we receive along the way.

The hidden God of Esther does not preclude divine activity but places God's presence within everyday causal relationships,

---

7   Jon Levinson, *Esther: A Commentary* (Louisville: Westminster/John Knox, 1997), 37.

8   For a sense of the apocryphal Esther, see http://www.biblestudytools.com/nrsa/additions-to-esther/1.html.

rather than as a savior from beyond. I believe that our spiritual practices open us to greater awareness of God's activities in our lives, but even here, divine guidance seldom gives us all the answers or a clear and unambiguous path to the future.

CHAPTER 7
THE FOOLISHNESS OF MEN

Esther can be read as a humorous account of the ways of men and their institutions. And, by "men," I mean males and not humankind as a whole. The three main male characters, including Mordecai, get caught up in their own dramas, putting themselves and their people at risk. Though the story has a happy ending, this is solely due to Esther taking charge of the situation, guiding the king to the right decision, eliminating Haman's threat, and challenging Mordecai to rally the people to avert disaster. Although Mordecai begins as Esther's mentor, protector, and advisor, Esther reverses their roles, becoming his spiritual and political advisor.

The story begins with King Ahasuerus hosting two drinking parties and bragfests, comprising 187 days and intended to show off the king's wealth and power. A third, less grandiose event is sponsored by the beautiful Queen Vashti. In the midst of the revels, the king requests Queen Vashti's attendance. He wants to show off his dearest possession, the beautiful queen, perhaps, as one Jewish tale suggests, wearing nothing but her crown. Vashti refuses and then all hell breaks loose. Already impaired to an abundance of wine, the king is enraged and his advisors point out that the social order will collapse if news of the queen's insubordination gets out to the women or the realm. In panic, his advisors assert that this deed "will be made known to all the women, causing them to look with contempt on their husbands" (1:17).

We don't know Vashti's reasons for refusing the king's request. Perhaps, she is enjoying her own party and sees no reason to sacrifice her role as hostess to stroke Ahasuerus' male ego. She may also find the idea of parading in front of a group of drunken men both objectifying and demeaning to her as a woman and queen.

There is a cost to Vashti's decision. Her defiance leads, first, to her dismissal as queen and then an edict stating that every man should be master of his own house. The king's advisors believe that Vashti's insubordination must be nipped in the bud before it spreads to the whole realm. Ironically, Ahasuerus's desire to shore up his fragile male ego by bureaucratic initiative spreads the news of his wife's disobedience throughout the realm.

After he has sobered up, Ahasuerus remembers Vashti and the pleasure she gave him. But, his edict is final and cannot be amended. Once again, the counselors get to work. The apparently well-run bureaucracy goes into high gear once again, rounding up the most beautiful women of every province. Even the king's romantic relationships must be managed by his advisors! Again, Ahasuerus seems to react to events rather than take charge in leading his nation. He leaves the difficult decisions to his advisors and rubber stamps whatever counsel they give him, whether it deals with his marriage, political affairs, romantic relationships, and later the fate of the Jews. Anyone with a legislative plan can use his royal signet ring!

Among those rounded up for the beauty contest is Esther or Hadassah. Already an orphan and exile from her homeland, she becomes a part of the king's harem, most likely against her will. Women are viewed as property, whose primary vocation is to support their husbands' delicate egos and provide pleasure and male offspring.

Enter Haman the Agagite, the king's closest political advisor. Puffed up by his rise to power, his joy is short-lived. His ego is so fragile that, despite his prominence, he is utterly deflated by Mordecai's refusal to bow down to him. While no reason is given for Mordecai's apparently defiant behavior, scholars have suggested a number of possibilities:

» As a Jew, Mordecai is forbidden from bowing down to a fellow mortal. Only God deserves our adoration.
» Mordecai is angry that Haman, rather than he, is appointed to be the king's adviser. After all, Mordecai foiled the plot to assassinate the king. He has yet to have received any acknowledgment of his heroism.
» Mordecai's refusal stems from bad blood between Haman the Agagite and Mordecai the Benjaminite's family. In the period of the judges, during the consolidation of the tribes of Israel, Saul refused to kill the king of Agag. His clemency led to Saul being stripped of his crown.

The angry Haman blows everything out of proportion and proposes another edict for the king's approval, the annihilation of the Jewish people. One man's insubordination must be punished by destroying the Jews. Haman's bruised ego leads him to enact the "final solution" for the Jewish people of Persia. While Mordecai is generally seen in a positive light in the book of Esther, his failure to compromise or simply absent himself from conflict with Haman places the Jewish people's existence in jeopardy.

Haman's disproportionate anger is his own undoing. Believing that he is due for the king's reward, Haman advises the king to give the chosen one the highest accolades, only to discover that these will go to Mordecai, whose role in preventing his assassination has come to the king's attention. Later, when Esther tells the king that Haman is responsible for endangering her and her people, Haman begs for mercy, throwing himself on Esther's couch. The king returns, observes Haman lying on the same couch where Esther is reclining and, believing he is trying to seduce the queen, has him hung on a seventy-foot-high gallows he had erected for Mordecai's hanging!

During the Purim festival, the book of Esther is read. Whenever Haman's name is mentioned, the gragger, a ratchet-like instrument, is played to drown out his name. What might have been the tragic destruction of the Jewish people becomes a comic opportunity for partying and inebriation, all of which is due to the foolishness of men, Haman's fragile ego and King Ahasuerus' malleability, arbitrariness, and leadership deficiencies.

The book of Esther recognizes the ambiguous power of governments. When leaders lack character or are ruled by their egos, governmental decisions can lead to the destruction of innocent people. The book of Esther challenges our own contemporary political gridlock and polarization and reminds us that political leadership is ultimately about service and promoting the greatest good and not defeating our opponents.

CHAPTER 8
FOR JUST SUCH A TIME AS THIS

Today, many of us seek to discover a thread of meaning in the course of our lives. We want to know our calling or have a sense that our lives make a difference not only to our immediate circle of friends and family but to our community and to the world. Both Ruth and Esther invite us to consider our personal vocations and their impact on others. In the midst of life, we don't always realize how one simple act can change the world. As I write this morning, I am listening to Christmas carols and looking forward to watching Frank Capra's *It's a Wonderful Life*, one of my annual rituals each Christmas season. One of the reasons this film inspires us is its affirmation that in the midst of our ordinary lives, simply doing what's right and responding faithfully to our families and vocational responsibilities, we can make an extraordinary difference to the world. Jewish mystics say that when you save one soul, you save the world because it is incomplete and unhealed until everyone realizes her or his identity as reflections of the divine. Our call in our ordinary lives is to be God's companions in healing the world.

The scriptures are a textbook in discovering your calling. When asked to stay in Nazareth and become the resident healer and rabbi, Jesus tells the townsfolk that he must go to other towns and preach God's good news, "for I was sent for this purpose" (Luke 4;43). Mary receives an angelic visitor and says "yes" to God's impossible vision. Perplexed and anxious Joseph has a dream, telling him not to be afraid, and to take Mary and her unborn child under his wing, protecting and nurturing them. A child hears that the crowd has nothing to eat and gives up his lunch, five loaves and two fish, and a multitude is filled through his generosity and Jesus' energy. In the Hebraic scriptures, although Jacob must continue wrestling with God, he receives his lifelong calling when he dreams of a ladder of angels, and discovers that "Beth-el," the gate of heaven is right where he is, and that a slick and crafty businessman like him can become the parent of a nation. Jeremiah protests his lack of preparation to speak for God and is told that God called him from the womb. Isaiah goes to the temple to find peace of mind in a time of national upheaval and encounters the God of the Universe, who asks "Whom shall I send?"

The question, "Whom shall I send?" is addressed to each of us in every moment of our lives, although some moments call for a clear decision between life and death, sobriety and addiction, and meaning and purposelessness. The nature of our calling is described by former Secretary General of the United Nations, Dag Hammarskjold:

> I don't know Who — or what — put the question, I don't know when it was put. I don't even remember answering. But at some moment I did answer Yes to Someone — or Something — and from that hour I was certain that existence is meaningful and that, therefore, my life, in self-surrender, had a goal.

The books of Ruth and Esther invite us to explore our own vocations and discover that, in the midst of everyday life, we may be asked to be God's companions in changing the world. We may be the answer to someone's prayer or the helping hand that brings salvation to a broken soul. We may not know how we got to this point, but in this holy moment, the meaning of our lives is revealed.

This was Esther's experience. Her life path was circuitous and painful. She lived as minority and exile. She was orphan, having lost her parents as a child. Against her will, she was rounded up to be part of the king's "beauty pageant," and then forced to live in the alien environment of the king's harem. Beneath the surface, however, coincidences, dare we call it providence, guided Esther's path to royalty. Events also called Mordecai to urge Esther to reveal her identity and destiny as a Jewish woman.

Few of us rush into significant life changes. My calling to the pastor of a congregation on Cape Cod came after days of prayer and reflection, and trusting my sense of God's presence and my need, despite challenges, to say "yes" to the Search Committee and leave my two grandchildren and their parents in Washington, DC where we had lived. Yet, within a year of my calling, my son and his family moved to Cape Cod, after my daughter-in-law secured a rare legal position on the Cape. God did not announce God's vision, but I see God's providential movements in spending weekday afternoons nurturing our two grandchildren.

When Mordecai asked Esther to come out of the closet and use her power and ethnicity to deliver the Jewish people from genocide, she didn't immediately say "yes." She knew that if the king were displeased, she might, according to law, be stripped of her crown and then killed. Her prudence is appropriate, but Mordecai believes that she must act soon or all will be lost. Undeterred by her prudence, Mordecai calls her to decision:

> *Do not think that in the king's palace you will escape any more than all the other Jews. For if you keep silence at such a time as this, relief and deliverance will rise for the Jews from another quarter, but you and your father's family will perish. Who knows? Perhaps you have come to royal dignity for just such a time as this.*
> — Esther 4:13–14

Esther knows that a decision must be made, but it cannot be made without prayer and reflection. As she ponders what to do, Esther begins to take charge. She orders Mordecai to have all the Jews in Susa, the royal city, begin a fast on her behalf. During that time, Esther and her royal court will also refrain from eating and drinking. Coming to the king unannounced is risky business, and Esther must be prepared for whatever outcome is in store for her. But, the moment that Esther says "yes" to her vocation, she becomes a transformed person. She finds meaning, courage, and claims her power and role as national leader:

» She becomes Mordecai's guide and commander.
» She risks her life.
» She devises a plan to save her people.
» She becomes a lawmaker.
» She becomes primary advisor to the king.

When Esther says "yes" to her calling, her life unfolds in dramatic and unexpected ways and she becomes a person of power and energy. Like Ruth, her agency leads to adventure and the well-being and survival of her people.

Esther challenges us to look for a gentle, often unnamed providence moving through our own lives. This providence calls us forward to new possibilities and gives us dreams of what we can be in partnership with God. This gentle providence does not coerce or compel, but invites and encourages. We can always say "no" and turn our backs on the highest possibilities available. But, when we say "yes," our lives are forever transformed. We find meaning, energy, and purpose.

In the Hebraic text of Esther, this providence remains unnamed as it moves through our life circumstances. Later, the apostle Paul was to see this providence in terms of our calling within the body of Christ, our communities of faith and the communities of life.

> *Now there are varieties of gifts, but the same Spirit; and there are varieties of services, but the same Lord; and there are varieties of activities, but it is the same God who activates all of them in everyone. To each is given the manifestation of the Spirit for the common good.*
>
> — 1 Corinthians 12:4–7

Our vocation emerges from the inspiration of God's Spirit. Our vocation is part of the ecology of our community and contributes to the health of ourselves and the whole. Our gifts are relational; they emerge in relationships and contribute to communities beyond ourselves. Our calling emerges where our gifts meet the world's needs, or as Frederick Buechner asserts, where your deep gladness and the world's deep hunger meet.

Esther found her calling through her careful and prayerful response to Mordecai's challenge. She discovered that in the midst of the challenges of her life as an orphan, alien, and surprising rise to power, that God had a vision for her life and that God had invited her to take the first steps on an adventure that would save her people. Our own callings are seldom as dramatic as Esther's, but we still are lured forward by possibilities, dreams, talents, intuitions, and encounters, through which God moves anonymously in our lives. There is no guarantee of success, but there is the promise of adventure and companionship with God.

Our vocation emerges in the interplay of God's call and our response. Here Esther is an example to us. Even in the Hebraic version, in which God remains hidden from Esther and Mordecai,

Esther takes some deliberate steps to discern her calling for just such a time as this. In the spirit of Jesus' words, first, she counts the cost of discipleship and following the path that lies ahead of her. There are risks but beyond the risk is the salvation of her people. Next, she takes time for fasting and reflection. She stills every voice, but the voice of vocation. She spends three days in preparation, opening to a divine wisdom greater than her own and awakening to courage to face whatever the future brings.

Throughout my writings, I have invoked the point-counter-point of words from Frederick Buechner and Parker Palmer: listen to your life and let your life speak. This is exactly what Esther did. For three days, she listened prayerfully. Whether or not she invoked God, she opened to a deeper wisdom and creativity, and considered how she might move ahead with her calling. Second, she let her life speak, adorning herself appropriate royalty and marriage in her time, and sought out the king.

This is the yin and yang of contemplation and action. Contemplation gives us guidance and a sense of our calling, and the rightness of the course we are to take. Action brings contemplation to fulfillment, saving our lives and the world by wise and welcoming involvement in changing the world.

CHAPTER 9
THE GREAT REVERSAL

The biblical story is full of surprises and reversals. Abraham and Sarah, well beyond child-bearing age, give birth to a nation. Their great grandson, Joseph, is left in a well by his envious brothers, hoping he will die slowly or be sold into slavery and rises to the political leadership in Egypt, enabling him to save his family from famine-related death. A Moabite widow, with no visible means of support, enters into a mixed marriage with a wealthy landowner and becomes the great grandparent of King David, the greatest of Israel's rulers. A mere shepherd, the youngest of his brothers, David defeats the giant Goliath and is later anointed king of Israel and leads the nation to the pinnacle of power and prosperity. Upon hearing God's call to preach to the city of Nineveh, Israel's archenemy, Jonah flees in the opposite direction, only to be swallowed by a great fish, and then brought back to his original destination, where much to his chagrin, the people of Nineveh repent and escape destruction.

Reversals of expectation are at the heart of the New Testament message as well. Jesus tells the parable of a Good Samaritan who risks life and limb to save the life of an injured Jew, despite the enmity between Jews and Samaritans. The often vacillating Peter, who denies that he knows Jesus on Good Friday, becomes the rock upon which God builds the church. Saul, hell-bent on persecuting the emerging Christian movement, encounters the Risen Christ on the road to Damascus, and becomes the leading evangelist to the Gentiles. Once an ardent champion of legalistic religion, Paul (formerly known as Saul) becomes the champion of God's unconditional grace, given to humankind apart from achievements and without legal demands. Unexpectedly pregnant through the movements of God's Spirit, Mary of Nazareth proclaims the wondrous and unexpected saving acts of God:

My soul glorifies the Lord, And my spirit rejoices in my Savior, For he has looked with favor upon the lowliness of his

servant.... He has brought down the powerful from their thrones,
And lifted up the lowly. He has filled the hungry with good things,
And sent the rich away empty.

— Luke 1:46–48; 52–53

The greatest reversal of all is the resurrection of Jesus, whose death on the cross is the prelude to glorious resurrection, thus insuring that God's everlasting life has the final victory over the forces of darkness and death.

The book of Esther involves a series of comic, yet serious, reversals. In the spirit of Joseph's response to his brothers, who abandoned him to be sold into slavery, the book of Esther reveals the truth: "Even though you intended to do harm to me, God intended it for good, in order to preserve a numerous people, as he is doing today" (Genesis 50:20).

The story of Esther tells the story of an orphan and alien who becomes queen. Haman the Agagite seeks to destroy the Jewish people and prepares a seventy foot gallows for Mordecai only to be hung on his own scaffold. Targeted for hanging by Haman, Mordecai takes over Haman's position following his enemy's hanging. The reticent Esther becomes a wise and powerful political leader. The persecuted Jews become a great people in Persia, safe and secure and feared by their enemies.

Providence puts into motion events that lead to reversals in power and prestige. Esther reminds us that within life's most difficult situations, a way toward the future can be found. The future is open, and limitations and setbacks can be the womb of glorious possibilities. Esther invites us to consider the following questions: What reversal do we need to claim? What event will turn everything around and place our feet on the high road to abundant life instead of the low road to death and diminishment?

CHAPTER 10
THE UNNAMED GOD

The book of Esther provides us with two contrasting ways of understanding the divine-human relationship. The Hebraic text portrays the human adventure as a journey without clear signposts. God is guiding us, but implicitly and indirectly. We discover God in the walking and not by doctrines or revelations. God's guidance is never obvious, but comes as we are going about our daily tasks, not from the outside, but from within the process itself. The more pious Greek text sees the divine human relationship emerging through our commitment to prayer and supplication. God is a force to be reckoned with, beyond our world and our machinations, yet working within the events of our lives, guiding them to their proper conclusion. When we pray, coincidences happen and a way to the future emerges. Still, in both visions, God is not — or chooses not — to be the sole actor in the history and personal life. God depends on us to bring about God's vision on earth as it is in heaven. Like a good parent, God gives us space to act and develop our own value systems.

Evils occur through plague, pestilence, individual hard-heartedness, and the actions of kings and political leaders. Suffering is both accidental, through being at the wrong place at the wrong time, for example, living in the path of a tornado or tsunami, and also as a result of human actions or passivity, for example, the interplay of Haman's hatred of Mordecai and the Jewish people and Ahasuerus' failure to take charge of his nation's policies. Regardless of the source of suffering, God invites people to become the primary agents of alleviating suffering and responding to institutional injustice.[9]

This interplay of divine call and human response was at the heart of Jesus' ministry. When he is asked whether a man's blindness is due to his or his parents' sin, Jesus challenges his followers to

---

9   Bruce Epperly, *Finding God in Suffering: A Journey with Job* (Gonzalez, FL: Energion Publications, 2014)

work while it is still light. On more than one occasion, Jesus told people who had experienced God's healing touch that their faith had made them whole.[10] Our task is to move from the sidelines to center stage to bring God's vision to the world. Inspired by God's vision, we act with courage and love as we "work out our salvation with fear and trembling; for it is God who is at work in you, enabling you both to will and to work for God's good pleasure" (Philippians 2:12–13). God is at work in every event, inspiring our quest for healing, wholeness, justice, and shalom; but we are God's primary agents in transforming the world.

Esther and Ruth are models for dynamic divine-human relationships. God wants us to act, and often waits for us to come to a decision, not wishing to abrogate our essential freedom. Our actions enable God's realm in the world to be advanced: a birth of a child leads to David becoming a king and eventually to the birth of Jesus, from the house of Jesse and David. Esther's faithfulness secures the survival and future adventures of God's "chosen people."

In everyday life and political decision-making, God is present but not at the helm. God does not micromanage, but invites us to maximal freedom and creativity congruent with God's vision of the whole. Apparently absent, God is nevertheless present in every moment, supporting our most creative and compassionate actions.

Ruth and Esther inspire our own agency. Neither they nor we look for miracles and divine rescue operations. We help create miracles in the surprising birth of a child and in the deliverance of a people from ethnic cleansing. They didn't wait for change to happen on its own; they took responsibility for bringing about the changes they — and God implicitly — desired. Today, in the spirit of Ruth and Esther, we are the change for which we wait, and the answers to others' prayers. By our faithful openness to greater vision, with no absolute guarantees, the world grows toward God's shalom, one act at a time.

---

10 Bruce Epperly, *Healing Marks: Healing and Spirituality in Mark's Gospel* (Gonzalez, FL: Energion Publications, 2013).

Texts for the Adventurous Reader

Bechtal, Carol. *Esther*. Louisville: Westminster/John Knox, 2001.

Beil, Timothy. *Esther*. Collegeville, MN: The Liturgical Press, 1999.

Brenner, Athalya. *A Feminist Companion to Ruth*. Sheffield, England: Sheffield Academic Press, 1993.

Fentress-Williams, Judy. *Ruth*. Nashville: Abingdon, 2012.

Fewell, Danna Nolan and David Miller Gunn. *Compromising Redemption: Relating Characters in the Book of Ruth*. Louisville: Westminster/John Knox, 1996.

James, Carolyn Custis. *The Gospel of Ruth: Loving God Enough to Break the Rules*. Grand Rapids: Zondervan, 2011.

Larkin, Katrina. *Ruth and Esther*. Sheffield, England: Sheffield Academic Press, 1996.

Linafelt, Todd. *Ruth*. Collegeville, MN: The Liturgical Press, 1999.

Levinson, John *Esther: A Commentary*. Louisville: Westminster/John Knox, 1997.

Sackenfeld, Katharine Doob. *Ruth*. Louisville: Westminster/John Knox, 1999.

Tull, Patricia. *Esther and Ruth*. Louisville: Westminster/John Knox, 2003.

QUESTIONS FOR CONVERSATION

The Book of Ruth

Focus: The Book of Ruth, Chapters 1–2 and *Ruth and Esther*, Chapters 1–2

Prayer: Begin your time together with silence and prayer.

1. Scholars are uncertain about the factuality of the books of Ruth and Esther. Can a biblical story be fictional and still inspirational and authoritative in its understanding of God and human existence?
2. Ruth is an immigration story. What does it tell us about attitudes toward immigrants and our own nation's response to immigrants? What moral guidance does it give us in relating to newcomers to our country?
3. What is your response to Ruth's vow? In what ways is her vow extraordinary? How does it shape the rest of the book?
4. In what way is Ruth's journey risky? In what ways is she a stranger in a strange land?
5. Is the description of Naomi as a "female Job" a fair one? How do you understand the problem of evil and suffering in human life? Do you think people deserve their suffering or that bad behavior leads to divine punishment?
6. Should people feel comfortable taking their grief and anger to God? Is appropriate to share the full range of our feelings with God?
7. Can you believe in God and yet doubt God's goodness or care for you?

Focus: The Book of Ruth, Chapters 3–4 and *Ruth and Esther*, Chapters 3–5

Prayer: Begin by considering times that you have experienced God's providence. Take a moment of silence and shout out your words of thanks and conclude with a prayer of thanksgiving.

1. How do you understand the relationship between romance and economic and personal security? What do you think of Naomi's and Ruth's motivations for seeking Boaz as a husband?
2. What happens between Ruth and Boaz on the threshing floor? What do you think of the allusions to sexuality in the text?
3. In what ways does Ruth take charge? What risks does she take? How does Boaz respond?
4. What do you think of Israel's social safety net — the practice of gleaning? How might these biblical economic principles be embodied in our time?
5. How does the story move from tragedy to a happy ending? Where do you see divine providence? In what ways is God active in the text? How do you understand God's activity in your life and the world?
6. What is the value the book of Ruth has for 21st century persons? What can we learn from the text?

The Book of Esther

SESSION ONE

Focus: The Book of Esther, Chapters 1–4 and *Ruth and Esther*, Chapters 6–7

Prayer: After a time of silence, lift up your prayers of gratitude and intercession for the world.

1) What do you think of the "two Esthers" described in Ruth and Esther, Chapter 1?
2) What is your reaction to Ahasuerus' drinking parties?
3) What is your response to Vashti's refusal? What are her motivations for refusing the king? How would you describe the men's fears that Vashti's behavior will threaten every household?
4) What do you think of the king's "beauty contest?" In what ways is it different from contemporary beauty contexts? If you were Esther, how would you have responded to the roundup?
5) What do you think about the feud between Mordecai and Haman? What do you think of Mordecai's possible reasons for refusing to bow? Are they justified? Is Haman justified in his response, basically, ethnic cleansing of the Jews?
6) What is your view of divine providence? What do you think of the idea of gentle, non-coercive providence?
7) What do you think of Mordecai's challenge that Esther has come to power for just such a time as this? Have you ever felt like you were at the right place at the right time?

SESSION TWO

Focus: The Book of Esther, Chapters 5–10 and *Ruth and Esther*, Chapters 8–10

Prayer: Begin with a reflection on places where you have experienced God in your life? Take time for silence and lift up prayers of gratitude for God's providence in your life.

1) In what ways does Esther move from passivity to action? How would you describe her personal and royal transformation?
2) How would you describe Haman's fall from grace? What do you think of the concept of reversal in Esther?
3) Why must Esther pass a law authorizing violence against enemies of the Jews? Is violence justified in responding to injustice or national threat?
4) What do you think of the coincidences in the book of Esther? Is coincidence another way of speaking of divine activity?
5) What do you think of the absence of God in the process of decision-making in Esther? In what ways does God actually show up in your decision making?
6) How do you understand the role of drinking in Esther? What is the point of the text's recognition that virtually every decision occurs under the influence?
7) In what ways can we be most attuned to God's vision for our lives? How do you discover your vocation?
8) What value do you think the book of Esther has for 21st century persons? What can we learn from the text?

... wise, honest, and liberating ....

—Patricia Adams Farmer
author of
Embracing a Beautiful God

Are you ready for the adventure?

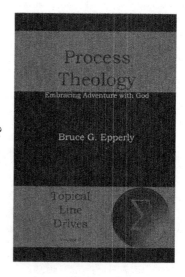

CPSIA information can be obtained
at www.ICGtesting.com
Printed in the USA
BVOW08s0957040118
504458BV00001B/63/P